SPINNING PLATES

Richie McCaffery

HappenStance

Poems © Richie McCaffery, 2012
Cover image © Gillian Rose, 2012
ISBN 978-1-905939-78-7
All rights reserved.

Acknowledgements:

Thanks to editors of the following magazines in which some of these poems were previously published: *The Dark Horse, The Delinquent, Drey, Envoi, HQ Magazine, Iota, The New Writer, The North, Northwords Now, Orbis, Other Poetry, Poetry Scotland, The Rialto, Smiths Knoll, Southlight.*

Ezines: *The Bow-Wow Shop; From Glasgow to Saturn; Ink, Sweat and Tears; Snakeskin; 3:AM.*

Printed by The Dolphin Press
www.dolphinpress.co.uk

Published in 2011 by Happen*Stance*,
21 Hatton Green, Glenrothes, Fife KY7 4SD
nell@happenstancepress.com
www.happenstancepress.com

Orders:
Individual pamphlets £4.00 (includes UK P&P).
Please make cheques payable to Happen*Stance* or order through PayPal in the website shop.

Contents

The professional / 5
Dedication / 6
The truth so far / 7
Arrival / 8
Mother / 9
Spinning plates / 10
Brother / 11
Piercing / 12
Tesserae / 13
Rust / 14
The rapture / 15
Two spoons / 16
Flotsam / 18
Late admiral / 19
Still / 20
Canna / 21
The collector / 22
Fairy pools / 23
Barney / 24
Ivories / 25
Ash / 26
Police whistle / 27
7 Pudden Wynd / 28

For Stef

The professional

You ask what I do for a living
and I don't think I can say.
There's something in the way
I take this teacup from you
without the tell-tale click
of ring on hot porcelain.

You ask, *Will this take long?*
Maybe. My questions must
be answered. Some are pointless
as wasps and the pain they give.
Others will take you many lungs
to satisfy the depth required.

Remember my dolphin smile,
my signature like snake-crossed sand.
You will notice some day soon
all your cups carry my trademark—
a faint hairline crack. I specialise
in subtle, half-bearable damage.

Dedication

In an underground copy
of *Lady Chatterley's Lover*
a shaky plum inscription:

'To Renee, my sweet—
from France via the Dunkirk
holocaust, 2/8/40, Sid'

All that way in a kitbag,
through panzers and snipers.
Bullets hitting the water
like kingfishers.

The truth so far

In the chalky trough under the blackboard,
lessons dusted and already forgotten.

The teacher is squawking away once more,
scratching into the *tabula rasa*

the truths so far about God and arithmetic
with the expungible white of fossil shells.

Arrival

When my mother arrived,
no one would sign for her,
left out like a parcel
on a stranger's doorstep.

Bundle of birth, fly-tipped,
swathed in a linen bag
stamped *Tate and Lyle Sugar*
seven lbs too heavy.

No mobile, just rain clouds,
her lips sapphire blue,
tiny lungs like strawberries
full of pneumonia.

Mother

An orphan, sixteen, with T-Rex pin badges
and homemade flares, she wades
to her bare waist in long wet grass.
A fallow graveyard of spent Victorian grief,
broken pillars, pink obelisks, Kestrel cans.

As her chipped blue finger nail traces
the golden genealogies, the baby
gives a sharp Geoff Hurst kick.
The anthology of wild flowers in her hand
won't go round all this standing granite.

Spinning plates

My mother was mad as mercury,
mad as a silken Disraeli stovepipe hat
hiding a gypsum-white rabbit.

She once told me—the malt talking—
I wasn't her first born boy;
there had been seminal drafts.

She said being pregnant
was like spinning a bone-china plate
on the thinnest stick inside you—

breakages were bound to occur.
It was a question of which piece
could drop intact and roll around

on a hardwood floor, its rim ringing
with cries. My sister is a wild firing,
an artisan's multi-coloured plate

still atwirl. I am a white canteen
saucer, ready to be tanned with tea-
slops. A cupped palm for spillage.

Brother

You could have dived to the wreck
on a lung full of air. I survived dinner
on only one bottle of burgundy.

You wore suits like a mountain wears trees.
I wear finer cuts no better than the hanger.
Today I am grief clad in obsidian wools.

Your shelf groans with dusty trophies.
You beat me in every sports-day race
and kept running into the laurelled gloaming.

Piercing

There is what looks like a spec of mica
on one side of her nose. Cubic zirconia,
diamond of neon amusement arcades.

She had money smouldering to spend
and a nose to pierce in this moribund
seaside town, this hen-night Riviera.

Wary of pain, she dosed herself well
with off-license paregoric. He punched
a hole in her skin like a clocked-off ticket.

She is not who she was. Alcohol
has danced over her in stilettos.
Still being roughly good, I'll go home

tonight and pray for her. *Patron Saint*
of ill-advised tipsy piercing, please cast
your balms and benisons on my mother.

Tesserae

She told me how she lost her first,
the ordeal in a 1970s avocado bathroom,

I thought of all the lost Roman mosaics,
tiny *tesserae* of vitreous gods

wearing pottery garlands of dead corn,
under the canola of Northumberland,

floorscapes of the great abandoned villas
hidden in soil too fertile for burial.

Rust

In the dunes at Warkworth beach,
wartime barbed wire corrodes
in marram grass, coiled like cilices.

All the gins in the Duke's woods
lie shut in leaf pulp, their teeth
stuck in a lockjaw of oxidation.

The languages I used to speak,
that ferric tang when you cough,
the staples in booklets that failed us.

The Rapture

Yesterday was Judgment Day.
We were stuck on an inter-city bus
in a traffic jam like a fleet of clippers
threaded through the neck of a cod's bottle,
an exodus on a single lane road.

Somewhere in God's granite allotment plots,
nanotechnologies of hatred and grudges
were stirring the blessed restful soil,
the dead limbering up for a carious dash
to the hot seat, stray dogs salivating.

Cars dropped in ditches like windowsill flies.
A petrol tanker was the first to run out of fuel.
The wind turned punk, a man began to cry,
stuck for hours, a busload bound for eternity
unable to stand each other for a sweaty evening.

Only those with a destination will be lost.
You woke and spoke of maybe next year
for your baby, coming off the pills for good.
My watch hit six and the light was snatched away
as raindrops danced like sperm on the window.

Two spoons

i
Making my umpteenth cup of tea
I grope the cutlery drawer and find
a caffeine-patinated teaspoon
marked 'hospital property'.

I have never knowingly pinched
from a hospital. I have no idea
how it found its way to my kitchen.
The old tenants perhaps?

They did leave under cloak of night,
though not through door or window.
I see a pale insomniac hand
in a waiting room absently slipping

this spoon in a pocket. Little lost
things are the detritus of distress.
Orphaned gloves, scarves, wallets,
teaspoons denote a mind

working beyond cold or comfort.
Scary to think the number of cups
of time-wasting tea this spoon
stirred. Now it's me brewing another,

listening to the tiny school bell of steel
on china, the quick *bonsai coriolis*.
I clutch the warmth both-handedly
and sip away at the seas between us.

ii
At the jumble sale I found a silver spoon,
a deserter from a service, left pearl black
after years of clammy hands, feeding its mystery
with runic markings all along its tapered handle.

Home and high from silver polish fumes
I revealed under the muck a tiny gilded bowl,
a Midas trick which pleased you, but jarred me.
The thought of what truth someone was forced
to swallow, to need so fine a spoon as that.

Flotsam

They found her faux-leather handbag first
with the usual tidal stuff, shore-froth, pincers,
bits of broken shells, ragworm casings.

It didn't contain the tools of her trade:
clot-red lippy, war-paint, a Stanley knife,
French-ticklers, a skint wallet of old plastics.

Somewhere, with lungs of brine and wet clothes
rippling as fins, she floated, eyes amphibious.
The tide was turning, they needed the boat.

Late admiral

It came in with the last of the logs,
a pod of *l'esprit de l'escalier*, a scabbed
unbirth, an unhatched chrysalis.

After a few days of inglenook glow,
a tiny miracle happened. In the frosty
Trossachs, a red admiral was born

in darkest winter, in a noisy pub,
a little but dazzling firework that went
off when no one was looking, an applause

of clapping red wings out of time with
the rest of the world's good deeds.
Enough to fan a dust mote from my eye.

Still

My toddler nephew found a dead mouse
in the park yesterday. He screamed and ran.
In life the little creature would have fled too—
fear is often a fair exchange of chemicals

but for once it held its ground, sure as stone,
the elderberry heart that once ticked as fast
as a lady's windup-watch now still, iron-willed.
The composure of its fur unnerved even me.

Canna

Island of lost chapels
congregated by swallows.

A broken pocket Bible
sits on a driftwood lectern
in tiny Rocket Kirk.

Sea wind cannot preach
more than its sting of salt.

Outside two lovers lie
boxed under marram grass.

The collector

Dead flies gather on the windowsill like raisins
and the dust, despite what Quentin Crisp said,
does get thicker after three years of indolence

in which time I've tried to decant the crust
from corked memories. The books multiply
in mitosis and remain unread, promissory notes

to myself that I'll have the time to finish them.
Things are starting to amount to a life. As a child
I collected Star Wars figures and stamps.

The little plastic aliens were my pliable friends
and the stamps, well-travelled artworks—best of all
the 1860s Andrew Jackson: Black Jack.

Decluttering at sixteen was my therapy.
The urge to collect seemed a need back then
to hold on to what's already lost.

Fairy pools

We pitched our tent that evening
in the basalt glower of the Cuillins
and went barefoot for firewood.
In the pines, in a fern glade
a burn ran like marbles over rocks.

Huddled around your pocket radio
at night, we danced blanketed.
A song called 'Secret Heart' came on.
Through hailstorms and squalls
a voice from the dark wavelengths.

I held you like a decanter
in the tent, pouring splashingly.
We were the only people alive.
I was all kaleidoscopes and adrenalin
and never told you it was my first time.

Barney

He collected postcards, old ones,
particularly from places bombed
or bulldozed, where street names
were just the hearsay of ghosts,
their stamps colourful shibboleths.

He'd vanish for days with no word
in search of those lost addresses.
Nowadays we wait for postcards
sent second-class from the night
and they always say *wish you were here*.

Ivories

For Theo Hedley's first birthday

He is as old as one new ring,
another inch in a tree trunk's waist.
Tonight Theo is teething, and sleep
is the downy stuff of dreams.
In the bloodshot morning, an ingot
of pure white is set in his pink gums.

The sun is a slow hydrogen bomb
detonating in the permafrosts of Alaska.
Netsukes of shattered Mammoth tusk
collect in zones of ablation. Ivories
appear from the unknown, with Theo
cutting his teeth on the bones of the cave.

Ash

i

All they brought over to Holy island
was a blazing torch, its flame flapped
like an elemental flag in the squalls.

The tidal causeway is under the sea
so we wait in the car as my grandfather
huddles into a giant pilaster.

He tries to light a rollie. After sparks
there's a hessonite glow to his drags.
He has six months of breath left.

ii

There is as much ash
in a smoked tab as there is
in a cremated finger.

The finger in question
was nicotine stained
and prone to point and jab.

God had a good long drag
on that one, then stubbed
it out in a rented ossuary.

Police whistle

In a drawer of his old ties
I find it, squat and silver—
my Grandfather's police whistle.

I blow it so loud and urgent
that even he hears in the dark
of his keyless oubliette

and with a great swooping
of mahogany truncheon
and gas lamps across dark moors,

a breaking of wax seals,
and questing of blood hounds,
all the unsolved crimes

of a hundred years are answered,
and justice is meted out
on the eardrums of passersby.

7 Pudden Wynd

When they built the house back in 1892,
someone put a dated stone escutcheon
upside down above the door.

I pass it every day and wonder
what it's like to live in a house
where time stands on its head.

Behind these mouldering bay windows
strange things must happen daily,
broken vases repairing themselves,

a place where the dead are anything but.
In the kitchen they try to un-bake stale bread.
Nothing is ever lost at this bat-eyed address

and I can't decide, from the outside
whether it's a blessing or a curse to never
be able to lose something, or someone.